## Bible Question Class Books

> # Bible Study Questions on
> ## Colossians and
> ## 1 & 2 Thessalonians
> ### by David E. Pratte

## A workbook suitable for Bible classes, family studies, or personal Bible study

### Available in print at
### www.lighttomypath.net/sales

*Bible Study Questions on Colossians and 1 & 2 Thessalonians:*
*A workbook suitable for Bible classes, family studies,*
*or personal Bible study*

© Copyright David E. Pratte, 2016
All rights reserved

ISBN-13: 978-1530582389
ISBN-10: 1530582385

**Printed books, booklets, and tracts available at**
**www.lighttomypath.net/sales**
**Free Bible study articles online at**
**www.gospelway.com**
**Free Bible courses online at**
**www.biblestudylessons.com**
**Free class books at**
**www.biblestudylessons.com/classbooks**
**Free commentaries on Bible books at**
**www.gospelway.com/commentary**
**Contact the author at**
**www.gospelway.com/comments**

**Note carefully: No teaching in any of our materials is intended or should ever be construed to justify or to in any way incite or encourage personal vengeance or physical violence against any person.**

**"He who glories, let him glory in the Lord"**
**– 1 Corinthians 1:31**

**Front Page Photo**

**The Agora (Marketplace) in Thessalonica**

"...and a great multitude of the devout Greeks, and not a few of the leading women, joined Paul and Silas. But the Jews who were not persuaded, becoming envious, took some of the evil men from the marketplace, and gathering a mob, set all the city in an uproar..." – Acts 17:4,5 (NKJV)

Photo credit: public domain via Wikimedia Commons

# Other Books by the Author

## Topical Bible Studies

*Growing a Godly Marriage & Raising Godly Children*
*Why Believe in God, Jesus, and the Bible? (evidences)*
*The God of the Bible (study of the Father, Son, and Holy Spirit)*
*Grace, Faith, and Obedience: The Gospel or Calvinism?*
*Kingdom of Christ: Future Millennium or Present Spiritual Reign?*
*Do Not Sin Against the Child: Abortion, Unborn Life, & the Bible*
*True Words of God: Bible Inspiration and Preservation*

## Commentaries on Bible Books

| | |
|---|---|
| *Genesis* | *Gospel of Mark* |
| *Joshua and Ruth* | *Gospel of John* |
| *Judges* | *Acts* |
| *1 Samuel* | *Ephesians* |
| *Ezra, Nehemiah, and Esther* | *Philippians and Colossians* |
| *Job* | *Hebrews* |
| *Proverbs* | |

## Bible Question Class Books

| | |
|---|---|
| *Genesis* | *Gospel of John* |
| *Joshua and Ruth* | *Acts* |
| *Judges* | *Romans* |
| *1 Samuel* | *1 Corinthians* |
| *Ezra, Nehemiah, and Esther* | *2 Corinthians and Galatians* |
| *Job* | *Ephesians and Philippians* |
| *Proverbs* | *Colossians, 1&2 Thessalonians* |
| *Isaiah* | *1 & 2 Timothy, Titus, Philemon* |
| *Gospel of Matthew* | *Hebrews* |
| *Gospel of Mark* | *General Epistles (James - Jude)* |
| *Gospel of Luke* | *Revelation* |

**Visit our website at <u>www.lighttomypath.net/sales</u> to see a current list of books in print.**

*Workbook on Colossians and 1 & 2 Thessalonians*

# Bible Study Questions on
# Colossians and 1 & 2 Thessalonians

Introduction:

This workbook was designed for Bible class study, family study, or personal study. The class book is suitable for teens and up. The questions contain minimal human commentary, but instead urge students to study to understand Scripture.

Enough questions are included for teachers to assign as many questions as they want for each study session. Studies may proceed at whatever speed and depth will best accomplish the needs of the students.

Questions labeled "think" are intended to encourage students to apply what they have learned. When questions refer to a map, students should consult maps in a Bible dictionary or similar reference work or in the back of their Bibles. (Note: My abbreviation "*b/c/v*" means "book, chapter, and verse.")

For class instruction, I urge teachers to assign the questions as homework so students come to class prepared. Then let class time consist of ***discussion*** that focuses on the Scriptures themselves. Let the teacher use other Scriptures, questions, applications, and comments to promote productive discussion, not just reading the questions to see whether they were answered "correctly." Please, do ***not*** let the class period consist primarily of the following: "Joe, will you answer number 1?" "Sue, what about number 2?" Etc.

I also urge students to emphasize the ***Bible*** teaching. Please, do not become bogged down over "What did the author mean by question #5?" My meaning is relatively unimportant. The issue is what the Bible says. Concentrate on the meaning and applications of Scripture. If a question helps promote Bible understanding, stay with it. If it becomes unproductive, move on.

The questions are not intended just to help students understand the Scriptures. They are also designed to help students learn good principles of Bible study. Good Bible study requires defining the meaning of keywords, studying parallel passages, explaining the meaning of the text clearly, making applications, and defending the truth as well as exposing religious error. I have included questions to encourage students to practice all these study principles.

Note that some questions on this book are more difficult and advanced. The study leader may want to skip some questions if he/she is teaching a less advanced study.

Finally, I encourage plain applications of the principles studied. God's word is written so souls may please God and have eternal life. Please study it with the respect and devotion it deserves!

For whatever good this material achieves, to God be the glory.

**Bible study commentary and notes to accompany some of our workbooks are available at www.lighttomypath.net/sales**

© David E. Pratte, November 13, 2016

---

**Workbooks, commentaries, and topical studies for sale in print at www.lighttomypath.net/sales**

**To join our mailing list to be informed of new books or special sales, contact the author at www.gospelway.com/comments**

---

# Assignments on Colossians 1

Please read the whole book of Colossians at least once as we study chapter 1. Answer the following questions on chap. 1.

1. Who wrote this letter, and to whom is it addressed – 1:1?

*Paul Gods Holy people- Saints*

2. List some things you know about Paul.

*Apostle chozen by God. He was called To Be the apostle of Jesus christ for the gentiles — Jew- and a citizen of Rome*

3. List some things you know about Timothy.

*He was a partner of Paul. He had a Jewish Mother + Greek father. Euning Ho By a christian Mother and grand mother*

4. **Special Assignment:** Study a Bible dictionary or similar book about the city of Colosse. List some things you learned.

5. After you have read the whole epistle, state the theme of the book.

*christ is lord of all including the invesible*

6. List some of the main points discussed in each chapter. *establishing that supreme authouy and preeminence of Jesus christ as the creator of all*

7. What position did Paul claim to have, and who gave it to him – 1:1?

*Apostle To the gentiles   Jesus*

8. Summarize the Bible teaching about apostles. What work did they do? What qualifications did they have, etc.?

*They were chozen by God To spread the message of Jesus Christ They were To establish Churches. To suring the gospel every whur*

9. List other **passages** about saints.

10. **Case Study:** Many people believe that saints are especially good Christians who died and have been appointed by a church so people can pray to them. How would you respond?

*The saints are those who au set apart for God. They have To Believe that Jesus died & Rose again.*

Page #5    *Workbook on Colossians and 1 & 2 Thessalonians*

11. What motivated Paul to pray for the Colossians – 1:3-5? (Think: Why is it important for Christians to pray for one another?)

12. List *passages* where faith, hope, and love are listed together in Scripture.

13. List some other *passages* about the importance of faith.

14. List some other *passages* about the importance of loving the brethren.

15. List other *passages* about the hope of Christians. Explain what this hope is.

16. What effect did the gospel have according to 1:6? What can we learn about how people can receive a proper understanding of God's grace?

17. *Define* grace and explain its importance in the gospel.

18. What does this show about the importance of the gospel and the need for teaching it? What should we learn?

19. *Special Assignment:* How far had the gospel been spread? Explain the significance of this in connection with Matthew 24:14; 28:19.

20. Who had taught the gospel to the Colossians – 1:7,8? How is he described? (Think: What can we learn from how the New Testament describes gospel preachers?)

21. What request did Paul make on behalf of the Colossians in 1:9?

22. **Define** knowledge, wisdom, and understanding. How do they differ?

23. What request did Paul make on behalf of the Colossians in 1:10? (Think: If a person is filled with knowledge, how can he increase in knowledge?)

24. **Application**: What does this show about our own goals in serving God? Is it possible to fully please God and be fruitful in every good work? Explain.

25. What blessings did Paul pray that they would receive in 1:11? List other **passages** about the strength God supplies for us.

26. **Define** patience and longsuffering. Explain why Christians need these qualities.

27. List other **passages** about joy and about thanksgiving – 1:11,12.

28. What inheritance do saints have – 1:12-14? How did we qualify to partake of it?

29. What is the power of darkness? Where does God place those who escape this power?

30. List other **passages** about the kingdom of Christ. Explain the relationship between the kingdom and the church.

31. **Application**: If these Christians were in the kingdom, what does this prove about the doctrine that the kingdom will not be established until Jesus' second coming? Can we be saved if we are not members of that kingdom? Explain.

32. **Define** redemption. Explain the role of Jesus' blood in redemption and forgiveness.

33. According to 1:15, what is the relationship between Christ and the invisible God? Explain the significance.

34. What is the relationship between Christ and creation? **Define** firstborn. (Think: Does this expression prove that Jesus was brought into existence by the Father? Explain.)

35. What things did Jesus create – 1:16? List **passages** about Jesus as Creator.

36. What is the relationship between Jesus and all the created things – 1:16,17?

37. **Application**: If Jesus created all things, then was He Himself created? What does this prove about the nature of Jesus? Is He created or eternal? Could the things said here be true of Him if He was anything less than Deity? Explain.

38. List other **passages** about the deity of Jesus.

39. What is the relationship between Christ and the church – 1:18? List other **passages** using this illustration. Explain the significance of the illustration.

40. **Application**: How many heads can one body have, and how many bodies can one head have? What applications does this have to the existence of modern denominations?

41. In what sense is Jesus the beginning, the firstborn from the dead?

42. **Define** preeminence. Explain how the context confirms Jesus' preeminence.

43. **Define** fullness. Explain the sense in which all fullness dwells in Jesus – 1:19.

44. **Define** reconcile. List other **passages** about reconciliation – 1:20-22.

45. Describe why we need reconciliation. In what sense were we enemies of God? What are the consequences?

46. How did Jesus bring about reconciliation? Explain how His sacrifice results in our reconciliation.

47. Contrast our condition after reconciliation (verse 22) to our condition before reconciliation (verse 21). Define the various terms used to describe our new condition.

48. What do our reconciled circumstances require of us – 1:23? Explain the terms involved, and describe what lessons we should learn.

49. **Case Study:** Some people teach that, when a sinner has been forgiven, he can never so sin as to be lost – "once saved always saved." What can we learn about this doctrine from the context we are studying?

50. List other **passages** about our need to remain faithful or showing that a child of God can so sin as to be lost.

51. How far had the gospel been spread at the time Paul wrote – compare verse 23 to verse 6? What does this show about our responsibility to teach God's word?

*Workbook on Colossians and 1 & 2 Thessalonians*

52. How did Paul view his sufferings – 1:24? Explain how one can have such an attitude. (Think: In what sense was Paul suffering for the Colossians?)

53. What illustration is again used to describe the relationship of Christ and the church? Where else has it been used? (Think: What was lacking in the afflictions of Christ, and how could Paul fill it up in his flesh?)

54. How did Paul describe his responsibility to preach the gospel – 1:25? *Define* minister and explain how it properly describes this responsibility.

55. *Define* stewardship and explain how it properly describes Paul's responsibility. What should we learn?

56. *Define* mystery – 1:26,27. List *passages* showing that the gospel is a mystery.

57. In what sense is the gospel a mystery? Is it impossible to understand? Explain.

58. In particular, what does this mystery reveal – 1:27? List other *passages*, including Old Testament references, showing that the gospel is for the Gentiles as well as Jews.

59. What is our relationship to Christ according to 1:27? List other *passages* and explain what it means for Christ to be in us.

60. What was Paul's goal in preaching and teaching according to 1:28,29? Explain what it means to preach Christ (compare 1:5,25).

61. How many people did Paul want to learn and obey the truth? List other *passages* showing that all people need the gospel.

62. *Application*: What do Paul's goals teach us about our responsibility in teaching?

# Assignments on Colossians 2

Please read the whole book of Colossians again as we study chapter 2. Answer the following questions on chap. 2.

1. What did Paul want the Colossians and Laodiceans to know – 2:1,2?

2. What was his goal or his purpose toward which he preached and labored – 2:2? What does he say would be necessary for their hearts to be knit together or united?

3. *Application*: Is a congregation united simply because they have a loving attitude toward one another? Is a congregation united simply because they have an understanding and knowledge of God's word? What should we learn about unity from this passage?

4. What treasures are hidden in Christ – 2:3? What does this tell us about where we should go to obtain these treasures?

5. *Application*: If all the treasures of wisdom and knowledge are hidden in Christ, what does this tell us about the nature of Christ? Could this be true if Christ were not deity?

6. What did Paul hope that wisdom, knowledge, and understanding (verses 2,3) would accomplish for the Colossians – 2:4? How does this show the importance of the proper source of spiritual teaching?

7. List other *passages* about the danger of deceit and false teaching in religion.

8. What does Paul say about his absence/presence – 2:5? In what did he rejoice? Explain.

9. What should we and the Colossians do according to 2:6? Explain the application.

10. What can Christ and faith in Him accomplish for us according to 2:7? In what should we abound? (Think: What should this teach us about the danger of other doctrines?)

*Workbook on Colossians and 1 & 2 Thessalonians*

11. What danger does Paul warn about in 2:8?

12. Explain the meaning of philosophy, tradition, and basic principles.

13. **Special Assignment:** What kind of philosophies and traditions does Paul warn against? Are all philosophies and traditions wrong? What lessons should we learn?

14. What position does Jesus hold according to 2:9? How does this relate to other descriptions of Jesus we have already studied in this letter?

15. **Define** fullness and Godhead.

16. List other **passages** about the deity of Jesus.

17. What position does Christ have according to 2:10? Where else is this taught?

18. What blessing do we have because of Christ – 2:10? What should we learn?

19. Explain the meaning of circumcision and the significance it had to Jews.

20. What circumcision should we receive – 2:11? How does this differ from Old Testament circumcision?

21. What is the relationship between baptism and Jesus' burial and resurrection – 2:12,13? Where else does the New Testament teach this?

22. Explain the relationship between baptism and faith in God's work. Is baptism a work of human merit by which we earn our salvation?

23. List other *passages* about the importance of baptism in our salvation. Are we saved by "faith only" without obedience to God, including baptism? Explain.

24. ***Case Study:*** Many people believe that baptism may be done by sprinkling or pouring. What we learn about this in 2:12? List other *passages* about the action of baptism.

25. What is our condition before baptism, and what does God do to solve the problem – 2:13? Explain the terms "dead" and "alive" as used here. Compare Ephesians 2:1-10.

26. What is the "the handwriting of requirements that was against us" – 2:14? What did Jesus do with it? (Think: In what sense was this law against us?)

27. List other *passages* about our relationship to the Old Testament law.

28. What did Jesus do with the principalities and powers – 2:15? (Think: To what principalities and powers does this refer? Compare Ephesians 6:12.)

29. What application does Paul make in 2:16 to the removal of the law as described in 2:14? What is meant by the reference to food and drink? What conclusion should we reach?

30. ***Application***: What is meant by a festival, a new moon, or sabbaths? (Note: Check Old Testament references where similar expressions are used together.) What application should be made to those who claim that we should still keep the seventh-day Sabbath today?

31. In what sense were these practices a shadow of things to come in contrast to the substance that is of Christ – 2:17? List other similar *passages*. (Think: What should we learn?)

32. What danger does Paul warn about in 2:18 that may cheat Christians of their reward? List other **passages** about whom we should or should not worship.

33. What is false humility? Explain how one can be puffed up while professing to be humble. (Think: What can we learn about the possibility of a Christian losing his reward?)

34. What does following these human doctrines do to our relationship to Jesus – 2:19? What does the Head do for the body that shows it is important to hold Him fast?

35. **Application**: Describe ways people can be guilty of failing to hold fast the Head, and give examples.

36. What should be our relationship to the basic principles of the world – 2:20? Where else have we read about these basic principles?

37. What applications should this have to following man-made rules and regulations? What did some of these rules and regulations say – 2:21?

38. How does Paul describe the nature of these rules in 2:22? What was the basic and primary problem with them?

39. How else does Paul describe these rules – 2:23? How were these rules useless?

40. **Application**: Does this mean the gospel has no rules that restrict what we may handle, touch, or taste? How do we distinguish proper rules from improper ones?

41. **Application**: Give some examples of modern-day rules in which man-made doctrines forbid touching, tasting, or handling, but the rules are not according to Christ's rules.

# Assignments on Colossians 3

Please read the whole book of Colossians again as we study chapter 3. Answer the following questions on chap. 3.

1. What things should we seek, and where should our minds or affections be set – 3:1,2? To whom is this instruction addressed? Explain the meaning.

2. List *passages* about the importance of spiritual as compared to material concerns.

3. Explain why the way our minds are set is so important in proper service to God.

4. *Application*: List examples that illustrate the importance of proper priorities.

5. List *passages* and discuss the significance of Jesus being at God's right hand.

6. Where else have we studied the concept that we died and were raised or given life through Christ – 3:3,4? Summarize what the book has taught about this.

7. In what sense is our life hidden with Christ? What is the significance in context?

8. What will be the consequence of this new life when Christ appears?

9. If we died (verse 3), what should happen with our earthly members – 3:5? Explain.

10. List and define each of the kinds of conduct listed in verse 5.

11. What consequence is caused by these kinds of conduct – 3:6? How did the Colossians relate in the past to this conduct – 3:7?

12. List and define other characteristics we should put away – 3:8.

13. Is anger always wrong? Proof? Why is anger a danger?

14. *Application*: List other passages about the dangers of improper speech, and describe examples of ways people are often wrong in their speech.

15. What form of improper speech should be eliminated according 3:9? Define it.

16. List other *passages* about lying.

17. What reason is given why we should put this off – 3:9,10? Explain the concept of the old man and the new man.

18. How is the new man different according 3:10? Explain lessons we should learn.

19. Explain the different categories of people that Paul lists in 3:11.

20. *Application*: Explain the sense in which none of these differences should exist in Christ. What lessons should we learn?

21. **Define** elect – 3:12. List **passages** that show that man has a choice and/or must meet conditions in order to be saved.

22. **Case Study:** Many people teach that God chooses who will or will not be saved unconditionally, regardless of man's will or choice. How would you respond to this view? Give illustrations showing that a choice or election can be conditional.

23. List each quality we should put on according to 3:12. **Define** each one, and list another **passage** about it.

24. Explain what it means to forbear or bear with one another – 3:13. Give examples that illustrate the application.

25. List other **passages** that teach us to be willing to forgive others.

26. **Application**: In what sense should we forgive others as Christ forgives us? Should we forgive others when they have not repented? Explain and prove your answer.

27. What else should we put on – 3:14? In what sense is this "above all things"?

28. In what sense is this the bond of perfection?

29. To what were we called – 3:15? Explain how one body relates to peace.

30. Where other quality do we need to please God according to 3:15? Explain why this is important. (See also verse 17.)

31. What form of worship is discussed in 3:16? Explain what the passage says that teaches us how to properly participate in this worship.

32. **Case Study:** Many churches use instrumental music. Does an instrument teach and admonish? Does it sing? Does it have grace in its heart? Does the New Testament passage teach us to use instruments in worship? What should we learn about instrumental music?

33. **Application:** Explain ways that people often fail to sing properly in worship.

34. What does it mean to act in Jesus' name – 3:17? How many things should we do in this way?

35. **Application:** List some ways that people often fail to act in the name of Jesus.

36. What instruction is given to wives in 3:18? List other passages that teach that the husband is the leader in the home and the wife should follow his lead.

37. List other relationships in which we must practice submission. (Think: Does submitting mean a person is less important or less valuable than those who have authority? Explain.)

38. What instruction is given to husbands in 3:19? What does it mean to not be bitter?

39. Explain the meaning of love. Give examples that show what love requires of us.

40. **Application:** Make applications and give examples that show what lessons husbands and wives should learn from the instructions in these verses.

41. What instruction is given to children in 3:20? List other **passages** that describe the responsibility of children to obey their parents or to learn from their instruction.

---

42. **Application**: Explain ways children benefit from the guidance of their parents.

---

43. What instruction is given to parents in 3:21? List other **passages** about the responsibilities of parents in training their children.

---

44. **Application**: List ways parents are sometimes guilty of provoking and discouraging their children in violation of the Scriptures.

---

45. Who is addressed in 3:22, and what are they instructed to do? List other **passages** about the responsibilities of servants and masters.

46. **Define** eyeservice and men-pleasers.

47. How do a servant's responsibilities to his master relate to his responsibilities to the Lord – 3:23-25? What is the significance?

48. List other **passages** describing the work ethic Christians should have on their jobs.

49. Who gives the ultimate reward that we receive for the work done in service on our jobs? What lessons should we learn?

50. **Define** partiality. Describe some ways that people sometimes receive or expect partiality on their jobs? (Think: What should we learn about God's judgment?)

---

51. **Application**: What should Christians learn from these instructions about responsibilities on their jobs?

---

*Workbook on Colossians and 1 & 2 Thessalonians*

# Assignments on Colossians 4

Please read the whole book of Colossians again as we study chapter 4. Answer the following questions on chap. 4.

1. Who is addressed in 4:1, and what instructions are they given?

2. What is meant by giving servants what is just and fair? Explain some applications this would have to masters.

3. In what sense do human masters have a higher Master? What should masters learn?

4. **Application**: What lessons should modern employers learn from this discussion of masters? What should we learn about the practice of slavery in general?

5. What practice does Paul urge in 4:2? What does it mean to be steadfast in prayer?

6. What should characterize our prayers according to 4:2? Explain the significance of watching in prayer.

7. List **passages** about thankfulness. Explain the importance of thanksgiving.

8. For whom did Paul ask prayers in 4:3,4? For what did he specifically want prayers?

9. What is the significance of an open door as Paul discusses here? What should we learn from this discussion about the responsibility of those who preach the gospel?

10. What can we learn from this discussion about the responsibility of those who support gospel preachers?

11. 4:5 discusses our relationship toward what kind of people? How should we conduct ourselves toward them? Give examples of applications.

12. Explain what it means to redeem the time (check other translations). Explain why it is important to use our time wisely.

13. What instruction about speech does Paul give him 4:6? List other *passages* about the importance of proper speech.

14. *Define* grace. What does the grace of God offer to mankind?

15. List other *passages* about salt in the life of a Christian. What lessons should we learn about our speech?

16. *Application*: List some proper applications of verse 6 regarding our speech. Does this mean we should keep quiet about sin? How does the grace of God treat people's sins?

17. Whom had Paul sent – 4:7? How is he described? List other *passages* about him.

18. For what purposes had Paul sent Tychicus to them – 4:7,8?

19. Whom else had Paul sent to them – 4:9? What else do we know about him according to other passages?

20. How is Aristarchus described in 4:10? List other *passages* about him.

21. Who else sent greetings to them according to 4:10? What information and instructions did Paul give about him?

22. List things that we know about Mark. List things we know about Barnabas.

23. Who sent greetings in 4:11? How does Paul describe these men?

24. Who greeted them according to 4:12? What else have we read about this man?

25. How does Paul describe this man in 4:12,13? What lessons can we learn from him?

26. Who sent their greetings according to 4:14? List some other things we know about these men.

27. What request did Paul make in 4:15? Where else do we read about Laodicea?

28. **Special Assignment:** What does 4:16 tell us about the circulation of Paul's letters? List lessons we can learn from this and other passages about how Paul's letters were used.

29. What instruction is given to Archippus in 4:17? What lessons can we learn?

30. How does Paul conclude the letter in 4:18? What is the significance of the fact that he concludes with a salutation in his own hand?

# Assignments on 1 Thessalonians 1

Please read the whole book of 1 Thessalonians at least once as we study chapter 1. Answer the following questions on chap. 1.

1. Who wrote this letter, and to whom is it addressed – 1:1?

*Paul and to the church in Thessalonians*

2. List some things you know about Paul.

*Paul was called by Jesus Christ He persecuted the Saints Because he thought He was doing right.*

3. List some things you know about Timothy.

*Timothy was the Son of Lois and Eunice He had Been Taught at an Early age about God*

4. List some things you know about Silvanus.

*He was a leader in the Early Church He traveled with Paul everywhere*

5. Where can we read about the establishment of the church in Thessalonica? Describe the history of the establishment of the church there.

*It was in Jerusalem*

6. **Special Assignment:** If possible, provide information about the city of Thessalonica. (Check Bible dictionaries or similar reference works for information.)

7. After you have read the whole epistle, state the theme of the book.

8. **Define** the word "church" and explain how the word is used in the New Testament.

*The church is the Body of church Its the Place where christian gather*

9. **Case Study:** Explain how the New Testament concept of the church differs from what many people today think about the church.

10. What did Paul remember about the Thessalonians when he prayed for them – 1:2,3?

*That they had stay Faithful*

11. **Case Study:** Some churches teach that we are saved by faith alone without works. Explain and prove the Bible teaching about the relationship between works and faith.

12. **Application**: Explain the relationship between love and labor. What lessons should we learn for our own service to God?

13. **Special Assignment:** Explain the relationship between patience and hope.

14. What else did Paul know about the church in Thessalonica – 1:4? List other **passages** about the New Testament teaching about election.

15. **Case Study:** Calvinism teaches we were unconditionally chosen by God to salvation or condemnation before the world began. Explain the New Testament teaching about election, and prove by Scripture whether it is conditional or unconditional.

16. How did the gospel come to the Thessalonians according to 1:5? Explain the significance of the gospel coming in word and in power.

17. Explain the significance of the gospel coming in the Holy Spirit and in assurance.

18. In what sense should Christians be followers of inspired teachers and of the Lord – 1:6? What can we learn about the importance of following Biblical examples?

19. How had the Thessalonians received the gospel? What affliction do we know about in the beginning of the church in Thessalonica? (Think: How can we have joy even in affliction?)

20. What had the Thessalonians done after they received the word – 1:7? List other *passages* about the example Christians should set.

21. *Application*: What lessons should we learn about our own examples?

22. Where had they made known the gospel – 1:8? Describe the regions referred to here (see a *map*).

23. List other *passages* about the importance of Christians teaching the gospel to others.

24. *Application*: What applications should we make about our responsibility to teach others?

25. What effect did the preaching of the gospel have among the Thessalonians – 1:9? What does this tell us about the background of the Christians in Thessalonica?

26. *Special Assignment:* List other *passages* about idolatry. What can we learn about the nature of the true God in comparison to idols?

27. For what were the Thessalonians waiting – 1:10? List other *passages* about Jesus' second coming.

28. What had God done for Jesus – 1:10? Why is this important to our salvation?

29. What has Jesus done that should lead us to serve Him according to 1:10?

# Assignments on 1 Thessalonians 2

Please read the whole book of 1 Thessalonians again as we study chapter 2. Answer the following questions on chap. 2.

1. How did Paul describe their coming to the Thessalonians in 2:1? Explain the sense in which this was true.

2. Describe the spiteful treatment they had received at Philippi. Give b/c/v.

3. Despite this shameful treatment, how had they taught in Thessalonica? What should we learn about our own teaching?

4. What did not characterize Paul's teaching – 2:3? Whose teaching often is characterized this way?

5. Define each of these characteristics. Why should they not characterize our teaching?

6. What does Paul state about the origin of his teaching in 2:4? Why is this important?

7. **Application**: Whom did Paul especially seek to please in his teaching? What lessons should we learn for our own teaching?

8. What else did not characterize the teaching of Paul – 2:5? Describe how teachers are sometimes guilty of these things.

9. What did not motivate Paul according to 2:6? List other related **passages**. (Think: How does this relate to verse 4?)

10. How did Paul treat them according to 2:7? Explain the illustration.

11. How devoted was Paul to their well-being – 2:8? What reason does he give for his concern for them? (Think: How had Paul demonstrated this degree of concern for them?)

12. What would the Thessalonians remember about Paul's conduct among them according to 2:9? Explain the meaning.

13. **Special Assignment:** List **passages** about how preachers may receive income. May they receive financial support from churches? Explain.

14. How did Paul behave himself among them according to 2:10? How did the Thessalonians know this to be true?

15. **Define** each of these terms Paul uses in verse 10 to describe his conduct. Why is such conduct important in Christians, especially those who teach the word?

16. What terms does Paul use in 2:11 to describe his teaching? What can we learn about the work of teachers?

17. What illustration does Paul use to describe his work in 2:11? Explain the illustration. (Think: Explain the connection to verse 7.)

18. What was the goal of Paul's teaching according to 2:12? What should we learn?

19. How had the Thessalonians received the word according to 2:13? List other **passages** that show the gospel is the word of God, not just the inventions of men.

20. **Application**: Why is it important to know the gospel is God's word, not just the word of men. What problems result when people fail to appreciate the gospel as God's word?

21. Whom did the Thessalonians imitate – 2:14? In what way did they imitate them?

22. What accusations did Paul make against the Judeans – 2:15?

23. List examples in which Jews were guilty of the things Paul accused them of here.

24. What did this subject have to do with the salvation of the Gentiles – 2:16? (Think: Why might the Jews have acted this way regarding the salvation of the Gentiles?)

25. How had Jews demonstrated this attitude when Paul was in Thessalonica?

26. In what sense was Paul separated from the Thessalonians – 2:17? What does he mean by this?

27. According to the account in Acts, what caused this separation? (Think: How would this have caused problems for the Christians in Thessalonica and caused concerns for Paul?)

28. What did Paul still want to do – 2:17,18? Why had he been unsuccessful?

29. Even now, how did Paul view the Thessalonians – 2:19,20? (Think: Why might Paul feel the need to reassure the Thessalonians this is how he viewed them?)

30. Explain the sense in which Paul's statements here would be true of his view of the Christians at Thessalonica.

# Assignments on 1 Thessalonians 3

Please read the whole book of 1 Thessalonians again as we study chapter 3. Answer the following questions on chap. 3.

1. What decision did Paul make – 3:1,2? Where was he at the time? (Think: Why would this decision have been difficult for Paul?)


2. How is Timothy described in 3:2? How does this differ from the way denominational preachers are often described today?


3. What reasons are given why Timothy was sent to Thessalonica – 3:2,3? Considering the circumstances of the church in Thessalonica, why was Timothy's visit important?


4. What can we learn from these verses about the work of gospel preachers?


5. **Application**: What can we learn from these verses about suffering for the cause of Christ – 3:3,4? In what sense is it true that we are appointed to this?


6. Explain why it is helpful for Christians to know ahead of time that the cause of Christ is going to require sacrifice and hardship.


7. According to 3:5, what concerns motivated Paul in sending Timothy? Explain.


8. What can we learn here about the possibility of a child of God so sinning as to be lost?


9. What can we learn from these verses about Satan and his work in our lives?


10. What report had Timothy brought about the Thessalonians – 3:6? How did the Thessalonians view the apostle Paul?

11. How did Paul respond to Timothy's report – 3:7? (Think: Why would this report have been so important to Paul?)

12. How important was the faithfulness of the Thessalonians to Paul – 3:8? What can we learn from this about the concern teachers should have for those that they teach?

13. How did Paul respond to the news Timothy brought about the Thessalonians – 3:9?

14. What prayer did Paul offer regarding the Thessalonians – 3:10? (Think: What can we learn about prayer from this verse?)

15. Based on what we know about the background of the Thessalonians, why might their faith have been lacking? Based on other Scriptures, how could Paul help perfect their faith?

16. What wish did Paul express in 3:11? How does this relate to verse 10?

17. What did he hope for them according to 3:12? (Think: Why had Paul emphasized throughout this section his care and concern for the Thessalonians?)

18. List other **passages** about the importance of Christians loving one another.

19. What hope did Paul express in 3:13? **Define** "blameless." Why is this quality important to Christians?

20. **Define** "holiness." Why is this quality important to Christians?

# Assignments on 1 Thessalonians 4

Please read the whole book of 1 Thessalonians again as we study chapter 4. Answer the following questions on chap. 4.

1. What exhortation did Paul give to the Thessalonians in 4:1? How did this relate to instructions that Paul had previously given them?

2. What goals should Christians pursue according to 4:1? Discuss the importance of pleasing God and of abounding in our walk for Him.

3. Of what were they aware – 4:2? What authority did Paul claim for his teachings?

4. In particular, what did the will of God require – 4:3? *Define* sanctification.

5. What conduct specifically must they avoid in order to please God and follow His will? Explain the importance of the instruction to abstain from such conduct.

6. List other *passages* about fornication.

---
7. *Special Assignment: Define* fornication. Give specific examples of what is required of us in order to abstain from fornication.

---

8. What vessel is referred to in 4:4? Explain what it means to possess your vessel in sanctification and honor.

9. Whose conduct should they avoid – 4:5? How does such conduct fit the definition of passion of lust?

10. Describe ways one might be guilty of defrauding his brother in this matter – 4:6?

11. What reason is given why we should avoid such conduct?

12. *Application*: Describe how our society fits the description here of the conduct of those who do not know God.

13. How does such conduct violate our calling – 4:7? Explain.

14. *Define* uncleanness and holiness.

15. What is the consequence of rejecting this teaching according to 4:8? What does this claim about the source and authority of Paul's teachings?

16. What subject does Paul introduce in 4:9? What does this say about their previous knowledge of the subject?

17. List other *passages* about love of the brethren.

18. Toward whom had the Thessalonians demonstrated love – 4:10? So what did Paul want them to do even though they did have love for the brethren?

19. How should Christians live – 4:11? What reasons are given for such a life – 4:12?

20. What does it mean to lead a quiet life? What characterizes a quiet life in contrast to one that is not quiet, as Paul refers to it here?

21. List other *passages* about meddling in the affairs of others. What problems can be caused by failing to mind one's own business?

22. *Application*: List other *passages* about the importance of working with one's hands. What consequences follow from laziness and idleness?

23. List other *passages* about the importance of a good influence on others. Give reasons why our conduct before the world matters.

24. What subject is discussed in 4:13-18? What is meant by those who are asleep?

25. What problems characterize those who are lost? Why do such people have reason for sorrow? (Think: Is Paul saying it is wrong to grieve when loved ones die? Explain.)

26. What assurance does Paul give about those who sleep in Jesus – 4:14? By what authority does he speak?

27. List other *passages* about the resurrection of the dead. How does our resurrection relate to that of Jesus?

28. In 4:15, what does Paul explain about those who have died as compared to those who still remain when Jesus returns? How might this reassure the Thessalonians? (Note: The word "prevent," as used in the KJV, has changed meanings. Check newer translations.)

29. How is the coming of the Lord described in 4:16? List other **passages** that describe Jesus' second coming.

30. What two groups of people are described in 4:15-17? Are lost sinners under consideration in this context, either dead or alive?

31. When Christ returns, what will happen to the dead in Christ – 4:16,17? What will happen to those who are still alive?

32. What will then be the destiny of those who have been raised from the dead or who are alive and meet the Lord? What does this tell us about the eternal destiny of the righteous?

33. List other **passages** that state the eternal destiny of those who are righteous.

34. What does the Bible say will happen to the earth when Jesus returns – 2 Peter 3:1-13? According to John 5:28,29 and Acts 24:15, when will the resurrection of the wicked be in relationship to the resurrection of the righteous?

35. **Case Study:** Premillennialists say these verses teach that the dead in Christ will be raised when Jesus returns, but the wicked dead will not be raised until a thousand years later. Prove whether or not this doctrine is correct, and explain what these verses really teach.

36. According to 4:18, what benefit can these teachings be to us? Explain how this gives us comfort.

# Assignments on 1 Thessalonians 5

Please read the whole book of 1 Thessalonians again as we study chapter 5. Answer the following questions on chap. 5.

1. What subject is discussed beginning in 5:1? To what does the expression "day of the Lord" refer – 5:2?

2. How is the coming of Jesus described in 5:2? Explain the point.

3. List other *passages* showing what the Bible teaches about when Jesus will come.

4. What will people be saying when Jesus comes – 5:3? What will come upon them instead? (Think: What people are referred to by the word "they" in this verse?)

5. Explain the illustration used in verse 3.

6. *Case Study:* Many teachers throughout recent history have tried to set dates for Jesus' return. What can we learn about such efforts according to Scripture?

7. What different group of people is described beginning in 5:4? How will this day affect them differently from others?

8. What makes the difference between how this day overtakes these two groups of people according to 5:5? What is meant by the expressions "sons of light" and "sons of the day"?

9. *Define* sober. Explain the significance in this context.

10. What lesson does Paul intend for us to learn according 5:6?

*Workbook on Colossians and 1 & 2 Thessalonians*

11. When do people usually sleep or get drunk – 5:7? Why?

12. In contrast, if we are of the day, what should we do – 5:8? How does this fit Paul's discussion in the context about light and darkness?

13. What protection should we put on – 5:8? What *passages* talk about spiritual armor?

14. **Special Assignment:** Explain how each of the qualities listed in verse 8 serves to protect us. Where else in Scripture do we find these three qualities listed together?

15. Explain the contrast between drunken in verse 7 and sober in verse 8. What secondary application can we make to drinking alcoholic beverages?

16. To what are we appointed and not appointed – 5:9? What did Christ do to make this possible – 5:10?

17. How does Paul describe the people who can benefit from this appointment of God in 5:10? How does this relate to the context?

18. What destiny should we receive through Christ – 5:10? Where will Christ live in eternity (note the connection to 4:17)?

19. **Special Assignment:** List other *passages* about the eternal destiny of the righteous. Use these passages to explain what that destiny will be.

20. Explain how a proper understanding of Jesus' coming benefits God's people – 5:11.

21. According to 5:12,13, whom should we recognize or esteem? What can we learn about the work that these people ought to do?

22. What group of people is Paul talking about here? List other *passages* that demonstrate your answer to be correct.

23. List the responsibilities that these people have according to the Scriptures. Prove your answers by Scripture.

24. Explain why these people deserve to be recognized and esteemed. What does Paul say about how Christians should relate to one another in 5:13?

25. **Special Assignment: Define** each of the categories of people listed in 5:14. For each one, describe how it should be treated.

26. What should characterize our treatment of all of these people? Why do all of these people need to be treated in this way?

27. How should we not treat anyone – 5:15? List other similar *passages*.

28. **Application**: Instead of taking personal vengeance, how should we treat others? What lessons should we learn, and how does this differ from most people's natural reaction?

29. What should always characterize us according to 5:16? Why would this be difficult for the Thessalonians under their circumstances?

30. List other *passages* about joy.

31. How does Paul describe our diligence in prayer in 5:17? List other *passages* that describe how frequently or how diligently we should pray.

---

32. **Application**: Does this passage teach that we must be praying 100 percent of the time? Prove your answer. Explain the proper application.

---

33. What quality should characterize our life according to 5:18? List other *passages* about the importance of giving thanks.

34. Explain the sense in which we can always be thankful. How could the Thessalonians be thankful even when they were being persecuted?

35. What instruction is given in 5:19? Explain how people might be guilty of this.

36. What is forbidden in 5:20? **Define** prophecy.

37. How might people despise prophecies? How does this relate to verse 19?

---

38. **Case Study:** Some people use passages like verses 19,20 to claim that spiritual gifts still exist today, and we are guilty of quenching the Spirit and despising prophecies if we deny these gifts still exist. How would you respond?

---

39. List translations of 5:21. Explain what it means to "prove all things" (KJV).

40. Explain what standard or what method we should use to put things to the test. List other similar *passages*.

41. What should we do when we determine something to be good – 5:21? What applications should we make?

42. What should we do when we determine something to be evil – 5:22? What applications should we make? (Note: Study this passage in various translations.)

43. **Define** sanctify – 5:23. List other **passages** that describe how we are sanctified.

44. When do we ultimately need to be blameless? What assurance do we have that God will help us toward that goal – 5:24?

45. What request did Paul make in 5:25? Why is it important to pray for those who preach the gospel?

46. How did Paul suggest that they greet one another in 5:26? List other similar **passages**.

47. List other **passages** elsewhere that describe kissing in ancient societies. What can we learn from these verses? (List other common forms of social customs from that day.)

---

48. **Special Assignment:** Is Paul here establishing a required ritual for Christians, or is he simply regulating an existing social custom? (Note: Compare 1 Peter 2:17. What if we have a president, instead of a king? Did other forms of acceptable greetings exist in those days?)

---

49. What did Paul want done according to 5:27? Why would this be important?

50. What can we learn about the nature of Scripture (the written word) from the way that it was used in the early church?

*Workbook on Colossians and 1 & 2 Thessalonians*

# Assignments on 2 Thessalonians 1

Please read the whole book of 2 Thessalonians at least once as we study chapter 1. Answer the following questions on chap. 1

1. Who wrote 2 Thessalonians – 1:1 (compare 1 Thessalonians)? Who was with him? (Think: Who is Silvanus? Compare 1 Thess. 1:1.)

2. To whom is the epistle addressed (compare 1 Thess. 1)? (Think: Review what is known about this church, and study when the letter was written.)

3. Skim the book and state its theme. Relate it to 1 Thessalonians.

4. For what did Paul give thanks – 1:3? Where else has he discussed their faith and love? (Think: What does this show about faith?)

5. List other **passages** about love of the brethren.

6. In what did Paul glory – 1:4? How might this relate to verse 3? (Think: In what sense is it proper to glory in people?)

7. **Define** "manifest." What was made manifest – 1:5? (Think: What was making this manifest? Study the context, especially verses 6,7, and explain how this can be true.)

8. For what did they suffer? For what should they seek to be worthy?

9. What is righteous for God to do (1:6; compare verse 5)? According to verses 6,7, who is being troubled (afflicted) now, and who will be later?

10. **Application**: Explain the sense in which it is righteous for God to do this. How would this knowledge help the Thessalonians?

11. List other passages about the punishment of the wicked.

12. **Case Study:** A friend says a loving God would never punish the wicked in eternity. How would you respond?

13. What do those who are now afflicted receive later - 1:7? When do they receive this?

14. List other **passages** about the second coming of Jesus. (Think: What passages say He will come with angels?)

15. Who will be punished when Jesus returns – 1:8,9?

16. **Application:** What application can be made of 1:8 to the doctrine of salvation by faith alone?

17. ***Define*** the terms: vengeance, punishment, destruction.

18. ***Case Study:*** Suppose you hear a preacher say that "destruction" means annihilation or complete non-existence, so the punishment of the wicked is that they will simply cease to exist. How would you respond? (Think: What is the significance of "from the face/presence of the Lord"?)

19. Summarize the punishment of the wicked.

20. When will these things happen – 1:10? What will believers do then?

21. ***Special Assignment:*** Explain how this passage would console people who wonder why good people suffer in life but other people seem to get away with evil?

22. For what did Paul pray in 1:11?

23. What is our calling? How many good works should we fulfill – 1:11?

24. What will be the result if we fulfill goodness and the work of faith – 1:12?

# Assignments on 2 Thessalonians 2

Please read the whole book of 2 Thessalonians at least once as we study chapter 2. Answer the following questions on chap. 2.

1. What subject is introduced in 2:1? What is meant by our gathering together to Him?

2. List other *passages* about Jesus' second coming. Where else is it discussed in 1 & 2 Thessalonians?

3. What belief did Paul warn them against (2:2; study other translations)? (Think: What had Paul taught in 1 Thessalonians about the time of Jesus' coming?)

4. What methods may have been used to trouble the Thessalonians? Explain them.

5. What event(s) does Paul predict must precede Jesus' coming – 2:3? (Think: What can we learn about the danger of deceit?)

6. List other *passages* about falling away or apostasy. Explain the idea involved.

7. What terms are used to describe the "man" involved in this falling away? *Define* and explain the significance. (Note: Please study the whole context before making specific application regarding who this "man" is and what "falling away" is described here.)

8. *Special Assignment:* As the study proceeds, make a list of characteristics of this "man" and the falling away. We will use this list to try to identify him/it.

9. What relationship does the "man" discussed here have to God – 2:4? What does this tell you about him? (Think: What is the temple of God? See parallel references.)

*Workbook on Colossians and 1 & 2 Thessalonians*

10. What does Paul remind them of in 2:5?

11. Why had the man of sin not been revealed already – 2:6? How long would this continue – 2:7?

12. What does 2:7 show about when this apostasy began?

13. **Define** "mystery" and "lawlessness" (or "iniquity"). What do we learn about the apostasy from these expressions?

14. What expression is used for the man of sin in 2:8,9?

---

15. **Special Assignment:** Connect verses 7-9 to verse 4. List some ways that one who is lawless might exalt himself above God or show himself that he is God.

---

16. Connect verse 8 to verses 6,7. When will the lawless one be revealed?

17. What will the Lord do to the lawless one?

18. What "coming" is referred to in 2:8? How does this relate to verses 1-3?

19. What will characterize the lawless one according to 2:9?

20. List Bible examples of lying wonders.

21. What is the purpose of miracles? How can one distinguish real miracles from lying miracles?

22. **Special Assignment:** Examine your summary of facts about this apostasy. List the possibilities of who/what it might refer to, and give evidence for each possibility.

23. What characteristic of the mystery of lawlessness is described in 2:10?

24. List other **passages** about the danger of deception and the deceptive methods of false teachers.

25. Why do people accept such false teachings – 2:10-12?

26. List other **passages** about the importance of truth.

27. What will be the destiny of those who accept these deceptions?

28. What will God send these people? Why?

29. **Special Assignment:** List other examples in which God used evil people for His purposes. Does He make people become evil? How could a good God send a delusion to people?

30. In contrast to 2:10-12, what did God do for some people in 2:13?

31. List other *passages* about how God chooses or elects people.

32. *Define* "sanctification." List other *passages*.

33. How are we called to be chosen for salvation – 2:14? Give other *passages* describing how this happens.

34. What do we receive as a result of this calling?

35. *Special Assignment:* According to the context and other passages, are we chosen to salvation conditionally or unconditionally. Prove you answer.

36. *Define* tradition. What did Paul say to do with it – 2:15?

37. List other *passages* about tradition.

38. *Special Assignment:* Summarize the Bible teaching about tradition, harmonizing verses that say to follow it with those that warn against it.

39. *Case Study:* The Catholic church claims that verse 15 justifies oral tradition as authority for church doctrine today. How would you respond?

40. What request did Paul make in 2:16,17? (Think: Why did the Thessalonians need to have hope and be established?)

# Assignments on 2 Thessalonians 3

Please read the whole book of 2 Thessalonians at least once as we study chapter 3. Answer the following questions on chap. 3.

1. For what should they pray – 3:1? Where else had Paul requested for prayers?

2. Study translations of 3:1. What should we want to happen to the gospel? Why?

3. From what kind of men did Paul hope to be delivered – 3:2? (Think: What kind of problems can such men cause?)

4. What will God do for His people – 3:3? Why is this important? (Think: Does this prove we cannot be lost? Explain.)

5. What confidence did Paul have in the Thessalonians – 3:4?

6. What qualities should we develop – 3:5? (Think: Why are these important?)

7. What instruction did Paul give in 3:6 (note the connection to 3:14,15)?

8. How did Paul emphasize the importance of this instruction?

9. **Special Assignment:** List other **passages** about church conduct toward members who sin. Summarize what they teach.

10. List other passages and translations that help explain the meaning of "withdraw" (compare verse 14). **Define** the word. (Think: Who breaks the "fellowship" — the church or the sinner? How is it broken? Compare 1 John 1:7. What does the church withdraw?)

11. From how many brethren should the church withdraw – 3:6? (Think: What do other passages say must be done before withdrawal?)


12. Here are passages that use various grammatical forms of "order" or "disorder" ("unruly") – you may wish to find others – 1 Thessalonians 5:14; 1 Corinthians 14:40; 16:1; Colossians 2:5; Acts 22:10 ("appointed"). **Define** "order" and "disorder."


13. **Special Assignment**: As we study 3:6-15, gather evidence to answer this question: Do verses 6,14,15 teach a **general** principle which is applied in verses 7—12 to a **specific** sin, or do verses 6,14,15 apply **only** to the specific sin of verses 7-12?


14. How else does 3:6 describe those who should be withdrawn from?


15. **Define** "tradition." Where else in 2 Thessalonians have we studied about it? How does verse 6 relate to the earlier references?


16. What kind of disorderly conduct is discussed in 3:7-12?


17. What example had Paul set – 3:8?


18. List other **passages** regarding Paul's labor with his hands. (Think: What "authority" does Paul refer to in verse 9?)


19. How should one be treated if he will not work – 3:10? How important is this instruction?


20. List other **passages** that require people to work.


21. **Application:** Explain and give examples of the application of verse 10.

22. What specific problem at Thessalonica concerned Paul – 3:11?

23. **Define** "busybody." Why is it often associated with idleness?

24. List other **passages** about busybodies or related sins. (Think: Does "disorderly" in 3:12 refer only to idleness? Is any other sin listed as an example of disorderly conduct? Explain.)

25. What correction should these non-working members make – 3:12?

26. What admonition does Paul give in 3:13? Why is this needed in context? List similar **passages**.

27. Who should be disciplined according to 3:14? Does this refer only to idleness?

28. Explain the meaning of "note" and "do not keep company." Check other translations and similar passages.

29. What effect do we hope this treatment will have on the sinner? Explain.

30. What additional conduct does 3:15 describe? What does this show about our motives? (Think: Complete your list of evidence whether verses 6-15 apply just to the sin of idleness or whether it teaches a general principle with many applications including idleness.)

31. How does Paul conclude the letter – 3:16-18? Why was a handwritten salutation important (compare 2:2)?

**Printed books, booklets, and tracts available at**
www.lighttomypath.net/sales
**Free Bible study articles online at**
www.gospelway.com
**Free Bible courses online at**
www.biblestudylessons.com
**Free class books at**
www.biblestudylessons.com/classbooks
**Free commentaries on Bible books at**
www.gospelway.com/commentary
**Contact the author at**
www.gospelway.com/comments
**Free e-mail Bible study newsletter at**
www.gospelway.com/update_subscribe.htm